Hey! Bill!

The dark art of anti-social selling (how and why not to do it)

by

Bill Palmer

Hey! Bill!

The dark art of anti-social selling

(and how and why not to do it)

ISBN: 9798731220279

First published in 2021

Table of Contents

Foreword

Introduction

    Social vs anti-social selling
    How to use this book

Part 1: How to fail – all too common mistakes

    1. At least buy me a drink first
    2. Empty gestures make least noise
    3. I'm an expert, really I am
    4. Ready, Fire, Aim
    5. TMI
    6. Full stop
    7. I can make you feel good
    8. When at the bottom of a hole

Part 2: How to succeed – or at least improve your chances

    9. Have you done your homework?
    10. Only Stalin could say this
    11. Say Cheese!
    12. Are you in the right job?

Afterword

Acknowledgements

About the Author

Foreword

Consider this. I'm in the City of London, on my way to a business meeting. I have just emerged from the underground, at Bank Station. I have a short walk to reach my destination, along Moorgate. It is a lovely, sunny day as I stroll around the imposing bulk of the Bank of England and make my way through the busy throng.

Just ahead, I catch sight of a "chugger" – you know, one of those "charity muggers" who, with relentless cheerfulness, attempt to sign up the unwary and guilt-burdened to a monthly direct debit to "benefit" some charity or another. Never mind that it takes the poor charity itself months to pay the debt they will owe to the chugger for their signing you up, it's for a good cause!

I do my bit already for a number of causes, so I sidestep and politely refuse the chugger's approach; they are so easy to spot with their hi-vis jackets, clipboards and rictus grins.

Suddenly a strange man appears in front of me from out of the crowd. I have no idea who he is – never seen him before in my life. He grabs me by the shoulders in a vice-like grip. There is no avoiding him.

He starts to speak; at first, I don't understand the words that tumble from his mouth, then I start to realise what is going on…

"IT'S NO WONDER THAT WITH SKY-HIGH SOFTWARE DEVELOPER SALARIES AND A SEVERE LACK OF QUALIFIED DEVELOPMENT RESOURCES ACROSS MOST HIGH-INCOME GEOGRAPHIES, BUSINESSES OF ALL SIZES ARE STRUGGLING TO COPE UP WITH

A FEW CHALLENGES INCLUDE - EXPERIENCING THE LACK OF SPECIFIC IN-HOUSE EXPERTISE; UNABLE TO FIND A SUITABLE LOCAL TALENT IN TIME; IN NEED OF SOME EXTRA RESOURCES FOR THE

GROWTH PURPOSE OR LOOKING TO MINIMIZE OPERATIONAL, INFRASTRUCTURAL, AND OTHER COSTS. HOW DO YOU THEN TACKLE THIS CHALLENGES?

WE HELP ORGANIZATIONS ACHIEVE MORE BY INVESTING LESS WITH OUR TECHNICAL EXPERTISE ON MULTIPLE FRONTS SUCH AS:

- FRONT END - OUR FRONT END DEVELOPERS CREATE TOP-NOTCH WEB APPLICATIONS AND WEB PAGES WITH THE HELP OF JAVASCRIPT, HTML, AND CSS, ETC.
- JAVASCRIPT /JQUERY; HTML / CSS; ANGULAR JS; REACT JS; VUE JS
- BACK-END - OUR BACKEND DEVELOPERS USE PHP & JS FRAMEWORKS ALONG WITH SUBSTANTIAL WORK MODULES AND ENGAGING MODELS TO DELIVER TOP-QUALITY BACKEND DEVELOPMENT SERVICES.

- JAVA; .NET CORE; .NET; PHP; NODE JS; PYTHON
- MOBILE - WE LEVERAGE CUTTING EDGE MOBILE TECHNOLOGIES LIKE ANDROID, FLUTTER, XAMARIN, IONIC, REACT NATIVE, IOS, AND MANY MORE TO CONVERT YOUR IDEAS INTO A ROBUST MOBILE APPLICATION.
- ANDROID; IOS – SWIFT AND OBJECTIVE C; FLUTTER; REACT NATIVE; XAMARIN; IONIC
- DATABASE - OUR DEVELOPERS HAVE EXPERTISE WHEN IT COMES TO WORKING ON POSTGRESQL, MARIADB, MONGODB, DB2, ORACLE12C, MYSQL, MICROSOFT SQL SERVER, AND MANY MORE.
- MONGO DB; POSTGRESQL; MYSQL; SQL SERVER; CASSANDRA; SQLITE
- DEVOPS - OUR DEDICATED PROFESSIONALS ARE ADEPT AT WORKING ON VARIOUS

SERVERS LIKE AMAZON AWS CLOUD, GOOGLE CLOUD, MICROSOFT AZURE CLOUD, AND OTHER DEDICATED SERVERS.

- AMAZON AWS CLOUD; MICROSOFT AZURE CLOUD; GOOGLE CLOUD; DEDICATED SERVER!"

Eventually, just before my ears start to bleed, my assailant pauses for breath. I raise a hand.

"Excuse me," I begin. "I have absolutely no idea who you are. I've never encountered you before in my life. You clearly have no understanding of me, or of what I or my companies do. You don't know what, if anything, I need, or might buy; you are completely ignorant of the fact that I am not in the slightest bit technical and that 90% of what you have just said is completely meaningless to me.

In short, you have not targeted, you have not qualified and you have not even taken the time to get to know the first thing about me."

Shocking, innit?

And yet that laundry list of verbal diarrhoea is a direct, word for word quote, complete with typos, from one of the 50-60 cold approaches I receive every week on LinkedIn.

What possesses presumably otherwise sensible individuals to think that they can win business like this? That a drenching with a torrent of irrelevant utter gibberish is going to lead somehow to a successful sale?

Read on…

Introduction

Let me take you back to an altogether simpler time, when lockdowns were only used by the authorities to quell prison riots and walking into a bank wearing a mask resulted in a ten-year stretch in said prison.

It was a time when the noble art of selling was practised largely face to face by people who had a modicum of training in the gentle art of persuasion and who understood that qualification means a bit more than a certificate for the 25-metre breaststroke. Social selling just meant buying your prospect a drink.

Into this gentle and bucolic scene, there arrived, on the 5th of May 2003, a new online platform called LinkedIn. Initially accessed only via the web, it moved with the times and launched a mobile app in 2008.

LinkedIn was created as a business-orientated networking tool and rapidly became a place where both recruiters and job-hunters gathered. Unlike dedicated job platforms, however, LinkedIn offered something more, something a bit different.

Right from the start, it became the de facto platform for business networking, with professionals from multiple markets and disciplines seeing the benefit of being able to find and connect with one another. Unlike its socially-orientated rival Facebook, LinkedIn was a place to do business, not to catch up on family matters or neighbourhood gossip.

LinkedIn, predictably, grew like Topsy. It met a need for people to network with other people in a work context. The company floated on the New York Stock Exchange in 2011. In 2016 it was acquired by Microsoft for the eye-watering price of $26.2 billion.

Over time, the original reasons for professionals to be on LinkedIn shifted; an increasing realisation that 740 million registered members across 150 countries worldwide (2021 figures) made it a target-rich environment and hence a magnet for any old muppet who thought that it was an easy route to B2B selling – big barrel, lots of fish. Today, LinkedIn is not the only professionally orientated social media platform, but it is by far the largest, and by far the most plagued by the phenomena described in this book.

And that's where our story really starts.

Social vs Anti-social selling

There are literally dozens of books and online courses that will teach you about social selling. Here's the Wikipedia definition:

"Social selling is the process of developing relationships as part of the sales process. Today this often takes place via social networks such as LinkedIn, Twitter, Facebook, and Pinterest, but can take place either online or offline.

Examples of social selling techniques include sharing relevant content, interacting directly with potential buyers and customers, personal branding, and social listening."

Lovely. What a great idea. It sounds like a really useful approach in the savvy sales professionals' kitbag. I particularly love the bit about *"developing relationships"* and *"either online or offline".* I'm also a big fan of *"sharing relevant content"* and of *"social listening".*

Nowhere in that definition does it mention hosing people down with irrelevant offers, sending "empty" connect requests or arguing bitterly when rebuffed, let alone repeatedly stalking victims, approaching the same people over and over again with the same aforementioned irrelevant offers.

That's the reality of LinkedIn today. *Anti-*social selling. Professionalism in sales is increasingly being replaced by "shouting" at random people, just like my friend in Moorgate.

All is not lost, however…

How to use this book

If you are one of those who, like me, are subject to a daily bombardment of drivel, you can simply regard this book as being here for your entertainment. I encourage you to read through, nod ruefully, laugh in disbelief and reflect upon the wilful stupidity and almost criminal lack of self-awareness of some of our fellow human beings.

If, on the other hand, if you are desperately trying to generate new business on LinkedIn and other social platforms and genuinely interested in learning how to win sustainable business and to use the tools available to you effectively, you might – just might – take some useful lessons onboard between the covers of this book.

For your convenience and reading pleasure, I have handily divided it into two sections:

Part 1 – How to fail

An exploration of some of the all-too-common mistakes that people make when trying to sell on LinkedIn and similar platforms. In order to illustrate each point, genuine, actual connect requests will be used – individual and company names will be changed to protect the senders from terminal embarrassment and shame – assuming, of course, that their EQ is high enough to feel shame…

Part 2 – How to succeed

Some straightforward, easy to understand strategies and approaches that may – just may – improve your hit rate – or at least stop you being reported as a spammer on a regular basis.

Part 1 – How to fail – all too common mistakes

1. At least buy me a drink first

The first of our seven deadly anti-social selling sins is overfamiliarity. I am the first to accept that this is entirely relative; there's absolutely nothing wrong with referring to a good friend as "Bumface" or "Fat Bastard" if that is within the context of your relationship, but if I have never met you before it's probably not the best thing in the world to start with a completely informal salutation – <u>you have not earned the right to do so</u>.

Now bear in mind that I am an English gentleman in my 50s. If anything, I'm a "Boomer", not a "Millennial" or a "Gen X" or "Z" or whatever other label the tooth-grindingly twee marketing people come up with to describe the next "wave".

"Hello" is a good start, "Hi" is fine. What isn't going to make me warm to you is:

"Hey Bill!"

"Aloha Bill"

"Yo! Palmer!"

…or indeed anything else that sounds like it should be accompanied by a tooth-grindingly enthusiastic high-five. It might work with your friends or your peer group, it might be your cultural norm, but it's *not* mine. If you want to sell to ME, you must first make some sort of effort to align with me…

…and the best way to start doing that is to READ MY DAMN PROFILE.

I have capitalised these four little words because they are IMPORTANT. There are many ways to get under the skin of your prospect thanks to social media, Companies House, Zoopla, YouTube, public sector transparency, etc, but if you are trying to social sell on LinkedIn then your starting point must surely be… shouldn't it…? your target's profile. They have taken time to write it, so the very least you can do is to take time to read it. Look for those little clues that warn you, "I'm wasting my time here" at least.

More of that later. For now, let's focus on rubbish approaches.

Once you have greeted me like a long-lost homie, your next mistake is wasting your time and mine by telling me just who you are. If your EQ is around your knees and your ego is so large that it has it's own weather system, this might surprise you, but the thing is, I can already see your name clearly above your connect request and – here is the really important thing…

I. Don't. Care.

That's not me being mean, but telling me who you are when I can read it already and when <u>I don't already know you</u> are completely and utterly pointless. You could be called Aladdin or Cleopatra, Brett or Mabel – it makes not one jot or iota of difference to my propensity to read your request and just makes you sound more than a little egocentric… oh, so it's all about you, is it?

Let's look at another real-life example to underscore this point.

"Hi Bill ! Great connecting with you. I can tell you are a busy professional. Do you have a fitness coach at the moment?"

By now, you should start to have an inkling how I am going to react to this approach from a self-confessed *"Fitness Coach, Model & Social Media Influencer"* but let's break it down for the benefit of the hard of thinking and those who see no harm in the words as written.

"Hi" – ok…

"*Bill !*" – oh dear… an exclamation mark. I'm getting the impression that you are the sort of person who laughs at their own jokes.

"*Great connecting with you.*" – oh lovely, a good, old fashioned, 1990's-style presumptive close. Plot well and truly lost by now. Let's plough on…

"*I can tell you are a busy professional…*" Can you now? So you are knocking on my door because…?

"Do you have a fitness coach at the moment?" Bang. Lost the room. Not only is this a closed question – one that it is easy for me to say no to – but it's of zero interest to me.

Goodbye.

Our friend has wasted his time.

And mine.

Which leads us to…

2. Empty gestures make least noise

There's an old saying that it is better to keep your mouth shut and appear a fool than open it and show that you are. However, this doesn't apply to business introductions. It is beyond me why anyone would simply fire in a connect request without at least taking a moment to explain their rationale.

It's Tuesday morning. I fire up my machine and find an empty request from someone totally irrelevant. Their "silence" speaks volumes…

BOOM! Here I am! Connect with ME me me me ME! I'm far too busy and important to tell you why. It's entirely up to you to do the legwork, to work out who I am, what I do and why I have chosen to connect with you, but that's because I'M IMPORTANT and you are just another SCALP!

Seriously, that's what goes through my mind. Worse, there are certain companies whose employees do this EVERY. SINGLE. TIME. A particular very well-known firm of independent financial advisers is a prime culprit. It has clearly been dinned into them in the induction that their BRAND alone opens doors, minds and wallets, that poor, benighted souls will be GRATEFUL to connect with them JUST BECAUSE!

Beware the empty request. More often than not, the seller is simply playing a lazy numbers game. But there is a more insidious threat; they don't want you, per se; they want access to your network… Yes, that's right. The network that you have spent time and effort curating and building for yourself, populated by serious, hardworking, handpicked professionals who won't appreciate it when one of their trusted connections is suddenly the indirect source of spam.

"Hey Bill, I see we both know Fred Smith – let's connect!"

No.

Let's not.

This is a bit like when your child goes to school and your partner says "let's invite all the parents of our child's new friends round for dinner!"

No.

Let's not.

See what I mean? Because we happen to have someone in common, that does not mean I will like, connect with or want to do business with you.

Have a reason to connect. State it. If I disagree with it, at least you have tried. Anything else is pointless, irritating and frankly condescending.

A close cousin of the empty request is a variant on the *"Be my friend because we both know Fred"* approach. The link is so tenuous it doesn't stand up to a nanosecond of coherent scrutiny.

Here's a genuine example together with my response.

"Hi Bill, I saw that you and I are both based in the UK and passionate about business! I always enjoy reaching out to like-minded business owners who have similar interests. It would be great to connect with you."

"Mr Smith,

At the last count, 66.65m people are "based in the UK" and there are approximately six million private businesses headquartered here. I am sure the vast majority of their owners are passionate about their businesses and a significant proportion have similar interests.

Please spend a little more time on qualification and targeting, not to mention reading my profile.

It's a no from me."

See what I mean? If you are going to claim a connection, make it a good one…

3. I'm an expert, really I am…

Back in the last millennium, when I was at school (I hated school…) there was a stupid joke doing the rounds. It was on a par with a knock-knock for its subtlety, but it appealed to a young lad who had just started wearing long trousers to school and was starting to be more interested in Doctor Who's assistants than in the Time Lord himself.

It went like this:

"What's the definition of an expert?"

> *I don't know, what is the definition of an expert?*

"Well, 'X' is the unknown quantity and 'spurt' is a drip under pressure."

Oh, how we laughed. In later years, older and wiser, I came to realise that nobody who is an expert in any field whatsoever actually uses the term to describe themselves. Personally, I take it one step further, generally preferring to think of myself as an amateur, doing things for the love of it.

This form of self-effacement is clearly deeply unpopular among those who anti-social sell. Self-proclaimed "experts" abound, along with their close relatives, the "professionals", and they will lose no time in telling you so.

As an aside, do you know the difference between confidence and arrogance? According to my Grandfather, a wise old man who survived two world wars and rowing his younger brother out to sea on a log, the difference was straightforward.

"A confident man knows what he can do.

An arrogant man never lets an opportunity pass to show the world what he can do."

He had a good point, and one that is wasted on people whose desperate word-salad taglines read like something produced from a buzzword generator powered by stale testosterone.

People genuinely write these, without the slightest trace of irony:

"I Help Corporate Executives Achieve their Dreams of Business Ownership by Offering FREE Franchise Advice, No Obligations!"

"I help business leaders catalyse their vision for a sustainable future."

"I Help Business Leaders Legally Avoid Taxes, Protect Their Assets And Become Their Own Bank."

Note, by the way, The Use Of Capitals… bit scary, but not half as scary as…

"⇨ Digital Marketing Expert | ⇨ Forex Trading Consultant | ⇨ Networking Specialist"

I can't help feeling that if this wasn't in black and white, it would be written in turquoise wax crayon. If nothing else, it reveals a worrying lack of focus...

I've kept the best until last. These three are great examples of my all-time favourite shoot-yourself-in-the-foot tagline:

"Email Marketing Expert at XXXX Ltd."

"Lead Generation Expert - I specialize in Linkedin Lead Generation for Business Coaches & Marketing Agencies."

And last but not least:

"We created a GAME CHANGING software that revolutionises LinkedIn"

Whoopee. Any one of the above is enough to make me run a mile. Looking at them together on a single page is making me feel slightly nauseous.

What on earth goes through people's minds when they write these things? It certainly can't be "I want to make a positive impression" or even "I don't want people to laugh at me".

Let's go back to just one of my favourites – the "Lead Generator" – one of the most pointlessly parasitic professions on the planet, on a par with estate agents, recruiters and used car salesmen. Here's a quiz for you. What do lead and demand generators, business growth specialists etc. have in common with fortune tellers?

They:

- tell you what you already know

- pretend to know something you don't
- rely upon your gullibility
- offer nothing for something

Harsh? Let's see... Both take your money with no guarantee of success. Lead generators and growth specialists both claim to have an unerring insight into where your next customer is coming from, whilst fortune tellers say they have an insight into where your dead granny has gone.

Let's be honest, there's no more a magic BizDev money tree than there is an afterlife.

In the same way, you don't see a crystal ball gazer winning the Euromillions jackpot every week, I have yet to meet a lead generator/business growth specialist willing to work strictly on risk-reward - no sale, no fee.

Funny that.

If they don't believe in themselves enough to benefit from their "skills" then why should we?

So why are they all over LinkedIn right now? Because they rely upon suckers being born every minute and on the desperation of all those business owners and leaders out there working hard to do anything to generate income in the wake of COVID.

I love the rich irony of being approached by someone who claims they can deliver me "qualified leads" when they can't even qualify me in the first place.

If you do think these people can help you, I have a bridge for sale.

4. Ready, FIRE, aim…

These three words sum up exactly what is wrong with 99.9% of the approaches I receive on LinkedIn every day. It's quite straightforward; if you are trying to sell me telesales, you will fail. If you are trying to sell me accountancy services, you will fail. If you are trying to sell me a virtual receptionist, you will fail. If you are trying to sell me your recruitment services you will fail. If you are trying to sell me your development skills, you will fail. If you are trying to sell me business development tools and techniques, you will fail. If you are trying to connect without an explanation as to why, you will fail.

Can you see the common thread that links all of the above?

You don't <u>know</u> me. You haven't taken the time to find out about me. You have either made assumptions without checking facts or you have simply not bothered; either way, the end result is the same. Because you have not made the slightest effort to tailor or target your approach to me, you will bounce off.

Hard.

Our military friends have an acronym - they love their acronyms nearly as much as old-school systems integrators - it's "OODA", which stands for Observe, Orient, Decide, Act.

The "OODA loop" is a useful way of approaching anything, from doing the weekly shop to closing multi-million-pound deals.

It breaks down as follows:

Observe - discover, research, study and learn. That last, "learn", comes in again later on – it's a *loop*, remember?

Orient – use your learnings and your experience (something that seems in desperately short supply in certain quarters) to relate the outcome you want to the outcome you are likely to get.

Decide on your next best action in sales terms, segment, qualify and plan.

Decide – another weak point for the anti-social sales brigade; it is as important to decide NOT to prosecute a sales motion (qualify out, in old money) as it is to choose to go ahead.

Again, judging by the piss-poor quality of the approaches I suffer, absolutely zero decisions are taken not to prosecute – it's much more fun to just spam people and it's cheap, innit?

Act – This is the kinetic bit. Pull that trigger, press that button, fire off that connect request. Oh… It didn't result in a sale… never mind, you can always go back around the OODA loop and LEARN from your failure…

…what do you mean, you don't learn? Clearly, there's no hope for you.

OODA is a good discipline for sales and business development people. Would you rather waste your time and mine, and occasionally - very, very occasionally - get a positive response by sheer chance, or would you rather think first then act with a higher proportion of success as a result?

Be a sniper, not a machine gunner. Ready, aim, fire, not ready, fire, aim. Don't sell stupid; sell smart.

Here's the perfect example of an anti-social seller who skipped every preliminary step and went straight to pulling the trigger; see if you can work out what gave him away…

"Hallo Bill, uw profiel komt al een tijdje te voorschijn als ideale connectie en ik dacht: "Connectie aanvragen en kijken of we voor elkaar iets kunnen betekenen."

I rest my case…

5. TMI…

You know those people you occasionally meet at parties and other gatherings who are determined to share with you every minute detail of their lives? Before you can draw breath, you are told what team they support and what car they drive (these, I admit, are almost exclusively male things), the names of their partner, their children, the dog, the cat, the chinchilla and three of what used to be four goldfish (I blame the cat).

Not one jot or iota of this sinks in because a) it is irrelevant and b) it is out of context. TMI, or Too Much Information, is a particularly modern blight, where everybody seems to think that they and what they have to say are interesting enough for everybody else to want to listen to them.

The anti-social selling equivalent of this is as follows:

"Hey, Bill I hope you are well! I understand that this time of year can be a busy time, so I'll keep it brief! I've been looking at your business website and I'm keen to understand how it currently fits into your lead generation strategy? XXXX identifies the anonymous businesses that visit your website, showing you the name of the business, how they found you, what pages they looked at and contact information for the decision-makers at those businesses! We have had great success in transforming our clients' websites into real revenue-drivers - helping them to achieve their business goals and a fast ROI. We'd love to do the same for you! Do you have a spare 20 minutes this week for a free online demonstration? We also offer a completely free trial, so you can see the results for yourself, before making any commitments! And as a thank you for your time, I'll send you a Starbucks voucher after your demonstration, so that you can have a coffee on us! :) Are you

free this week to discuss? What's the best way to reach you? All the best!"

Upon receiving and reading this carriage-return free zone, it's fair to say that I felt a bit like I had just had my leg shagged by an over-amorous Yorkshire Terrier. The cringe-making over-familiarity, the breathless questions, the use of exclamation marks!!

The icing on the cake is the offer to send me a Starbucks voucher as a "reward". Remember, this is supposed to be a business approach on a B2B networking site, not an offer to buy saucepans. In any event, I don't know a single person who would be motivated to do anything at all beyond retch slightly at the very thought of a brew from Messrs. Starbuck…

Just for fun, let me redact all the pointless puff in the above and reprint it. Let's see what we get left with:

Yup, that's right. Absolutely nothing at all.
Here's another:

*"Hello Bill, How are you doing? I am a
Transformational Life Coach and can
give you the power to upgrade your life;
whether it is in your career, relationships,
confidence, anxiety, family or finances.
Visit my website for a free discovery call
www.link Thanks"*

Don't you just love that phrase *"…can
give you the power to upgrade your life."*
It's so downright cheesy it belongs under
the grill on a piece of toast.

As an aside, most but by no means all of the worst culprits for TMI hail from the United States. It's a cultural thing, I know, but the point is, it's not *my* culture. Again, if you want to do business with me, you must align with me, not expect me to do the work to align with you.

Here's a particularly amusing one from across the pond:

"Hey Bill, it's a great day for new connections here in the world of Linkedin.

Great connections make the experience all the better and I've got room for great minds in my network; how about you?

Brilliance attracts brilliance and together we shine bright.

Let's connect!

Cheers,"

…needless to say, I didn't.

6. Full stop…

This chapter is all about the gentle art of the closed question. It takes a number of forms. Let's turn to our anti-social sellers to find some shockers:

"Hi Bill, Saw your profile on my LinkedIn feed and I wanted to touch base around sharing a free e-book of 10 Proven LinkedIn outreach templates from TOP INFLUENCERS. It can definitely help you acquire warm leads in less than a week. Interested?"

No.

Of course I'm not. Not only has this chap committed the sales faux pas of asking a closed question, he is also one of the self-proclaimed "experts" that I identified in chapter 3 above – in his case, his claimed expertise lies in my favourite bullshit con, lead generation...

Quite clearly not. Apart from the closed question, he deserves our pity for cliches and unsubstantiated hyperbole such as *"touch base"*, *"proven"*, SHOUTY CAPITALS and *"definitely"*.

Let's look at a few more:

"Bill - noticed you're in London as well

I run a program designed to help Execs lose their last 10lbs/add lean muscle and tone up (whatever makes sense for you)--even w/ 16hr workdays/no gym access.

Let me know if that sounds interesting at all!"

I'm not in London… nothing on my profile says I'm in London, and nine million people live there – chances of us forming a lasting kinship under these circumstances… nil.

Interesting value proposition? Nope. Why on earth would I entrust my fitness to some total stranger whose grasp of geography is so poor that his location of record is actually 98.2 miles from the aforementioned London?

But here's the killer… *"Let me know if that sounds interesting at all!"* The exclamation mark doesn't help, but the key point is that this is one of the worst possible closed questions – one that says:

"I have absolutely zero idea if my value proposition is relevant or interesting to you so I'll prove my stupidity by asking a dumb, closed question."

sigh

Shall we continue?

"Hey! Bill, I just went through your profile and it really caught my attention, We work in the same industry! It would be great to have you as a connection."

Yes, my friend, but it would not be great to have *you* as a connection… Again, breathless exclamation marks, lying (he clearly hasn't been through my profile as evidenced by the fact that no, we don't work in the same industry (an attempt at familiarity doomed to failure in any event).

The real error here is projection – *"…it would be great to have you as a connection"* may convince a four-year-old in the playground *("will you be my friend?")*, but it cuts no ice on a B2B basis.

Here's another:

"Hope you don't mind me reaching out.

With many public hospitals facing cashflow issues from the pandemic, several are now asking about our unique stock loans.

By the look of your profile, Bill, I thought your company might be interested?

Do you have a suitable email?"

Yes, I mind you reaching out, particularly since, for some reason best known to yourself, you appear to think I run a hospital.

In the United States.

No, I don't have a suitable email…

"Hey Bill, You may find this valuable. We provide a virtual digital media team to business leaders. Advantages over free-lancers or internal teams? Consistency, award-winning quality, scalability, lower costs, exceptional customer care. Would you like to learn more?"

Nope.

You're getting the idea by now, I'm sure.

Let's finish this chapter with a real cracker:

"Hey Bill, I manage global sales and development at XXXX. XXXX is focused on design and development, with expertise is in Web dev, Mobile app/game dev, AR/VR app/game dev, Blockchain dev. www.link I am interested to know if you generally believe in outsourcing?"

I just love this one for so many reasons. It's badly written, it hoses me down with irrelevant jargon, it is about as well targeted as a punch swung in a Dublin bar at 11pm on a Friday night and it asks the most ridiculous question imaginable.

Honestly, who knew that outsourcing was a matter of faith? As a card-carrying agnostic, I'm wondering if those who answer yes to this question gather for a weekly worship.

The lesson is simple. Never ask me something I can easily say no to.

Because I will.

7. I can make you feel good…

"Let me make you feel good
I can make you feel good
Let me make you feel good
I can make you feel good"

So sang Shalamar all the way back in 1982. As a sales technique, it's a goodie. Make your prospect feel good about themselves and their propensity to co-operate may well increase. Who, after all, doesn't feel their mood lift when they are made to feel special?

Which makes these tin-eared, low-EQ approaches from our anti-social sellers all the more inexplicable.

"Hi, I stumbled across your profile here on LinkedIn. Hopefully, our connection could grow until something mutually beneficial. I promise I have nothing to sell you. □"

"I stumbled across…".

Really?

What am I, a leg sticking out into the aisle on the train? Feeling really special, now.

"Hopefully our connection could grow…"

Ah – nothing specific in mind then. I haven't been qualified or targeted.

"I promise I have nothing to sell you." – I bet you say that to all the boys.

That smiley face is the final straw; I hadn't realised that 12-year-olds were solution selling these days; clearly, spammers, like policemen, just keep getting younger.

Whilst I'm on the subject, *"I stumbled across…"* is bad enough. The frequently used *"I came across…"* makes me feel more than slightly queasy.

Don't do it.

"Hello Bill , I was randomly visiting your website and found similar interest in

Information Technology, so I thought we should connect and talk about Partnership Opportunity. Kindly let me know your convenience for 15mins of Skype/Zoom meeting this week."

"Randomly visiting…" Wow. Need I say more? Actually, I will, just to make a specific point. It isn't hard to establish that I have more than one company and more than one website. Don't try and tell me that you have researched when you clearly haven't. It's funny how many anti-social sellers go deathly quiet when asked the simple question, "Which of my websites, exactly…?"

Let's finish this chapter with another absolute corker:

"Hey Bill! I hope that your staying positive and testing negative! We've never met, but your profile came up on my LinkedIn. I'm really impressed with your

background at XXXX Limited and would like to invite you to my network."

By now, gentle reader, you should be able to chorus along with me as I call out all the things that are wrong with this one.

"Hey Bill!" High five bro!

"I hope that your staying positive and testing negative!" One of the worst things to result from the pandemic (apart from the teeth-grindingly trite "the new normal" – it's the *next* normal, ask anyone who has lived through any macro-economic upheaval since the last ice age...) is the appearance of this ghastly phrase. It wasn't funny the first dozen times – stop using it.

Embedded within is another pet peeve. If you don't know the difference between "your" and "you're", or "there", "their" and "they're", back away from the keyboard and find a grown-up to ask.

"We've never met..." So why are you bothering me?

"I'm really impressed with your background…" Are you now? So be <u>specific</u>. Prove to me that you know what my background is. Tell me what impressed you and why, and how it relates to your pitch.

"…like to invite you to my network." Ah, there's that killer again. I'm far more important than you, so it will enrich your pathetic little life if you accept my gracious offer to link with me.

Oh please.

8. When at the bottom of a hole…

I know I said at the outset that there are seven deadly anti-social selling sins, but I lied – and this one is just too good to miss.

The first law of holes has an appropriately patchy history. In its simplest form, it is usually expressed as follows:

"When you find yourself in a hole, stop digging."

It has been variously credited to a journalist writing in the Washington Post, an American politician named Bill Brock and a British parliamentarian, Denis Healy. Since I am myself British, I'm naturally inclined to accept the Healy credit, but since I have lived under Labour when Mr Healy was Chancellor of the Exchequer, I'll go with the Washington Post version.

Applying this wise aphorism to anti-social selling is quite straightforward. When your untargeted, unqualified, badly written connect request has been rebuffed, don't be surprised and above all, don't argue. It won't win you business and it certainly won't win you friends. It won't even make you feel better.

Those most inclined to argue are those with the largest egos; we all know that sales and egos go hand in hand like cheese and Marmite, but like Marmite, if you allow an ego to build up in a small space, it becomes more than a little unpalatable.

Get your popcorn; here come the examples:

"I just let you know we have an offer going on. Surely you want to know???"

Nope. Because it is slightly less relevant to me than news of Barbie's AW collection. Oh - and I don't care how many question marks you use, I'm still not going to buy from you.

Here's another, together with my response:

"Hi Bill,

Very keen to discuss ways we can help you scale your tech team. Let's connect here and discuss further."

"Mr. XXXX,

You have neither qualified nor targeted. You have zero idea whether I have a "tech team" or what they do, let alone whether I require them to scale. Above all, you clearly have not even read my profile.

Let's not connect, and let's not discuss further."

"Hi Bill - sorry to upset you, but this was a targeted out-reach. I was hoping to speak to someone in your company who might be looking to bring in additional developers. We work with over 25 nearshore firms who we match with your specific requirements."

Firstly, I'm not "upset" – this is a common rebuttal. It's a take on "It's not me, it's you." Denial is generally rife among anti-social sellers – "I've done nothing wrong, so if you don't want me to sell at you, it's your problem."

Secondly and astonishingly, he's still trying to sell. I've said no, in no uncertain terms.

No means no. Qualify out, mate; don't try to justify the unjustifiable.

Last but by no means least, and again the arrogance is breath-taking, *"…we match with your specific requirements."*

No you don't, and that is the key point. You have reached out blindly, missed the mark, I have told you so, and you are still trying to convince me that you can meet my specific requirements?

The anti-social seller is never short on misplaced confidence. What they are generally woefully lacking is the simple ability to listen and learn. Situational awareness is a survival trait as well as a sales technique. If you aren't going to pay attention to what I say when I tell you I'm not interested, how on earth do you think I feel about trusting you to pay attention to my actual requirements?

My all-time favourite exchange is too damn long to replay here, so I shall summarise. Suffice to say I was approached by a hard-sell car dealer:

"I see you, Bill, behind the wheel of a brand new Merc – or maybe a Beemer."

Really? I wouldn't be seen dead behind the wheel of a BMW…

"I can put you in the car of your dreams, within the week."

And so on.

I pointed out – firmly – that I had no need of the gentleman's services, that I was not interested in his offers and that he was wasting his time. The reaction was – memorable.

"Why not? We offer the best deals around."

"What sort of businessman are you that you don't want the best from the best?"

"I put dozens of guys like you in their dream cars every month."

"I can deliver to your door."

He finally shut up when I pointed out that he was based in New York and I live in The South of England... Strangely enough, he went very quiet when I asked if he would ship "the car of my dreams" across the Atlantic.

Finally, there's something else that I'll put under this heading. It's not strictly arguing per se, but it certainly is a prime case of not listening and of missing the point by a country mile.

Follow this exchange:

"Hello Bill,

I am expanding my LinkedIn professional network. If you are open to a new connection, then we can connect.

Thanks,"

"Good luck with that, XXXX. I suggest you read my profile, then you should understand why we won't be connecting."

"Hi Bill.....I agree, New marketing company error. Messages should be: I help people leave their dead end employment and enjoy the financial rewards and independence of individual business ownership. My service is FREE to my clients.

I think we should go back to the above for non-visa clients.

For people in other countries I suggest :

I provide professional services for people seeking a non-immigrant investment E-2 visa. I represent hundreds of franchises and businesses that will qualify them to live and operate their business in the United States. My service is Free to my clients."

That whooshing sound is the anti-social seller in question missing the point. I could also have filed this under TMI, I suppose, but either way, it's a splendid example of a low-EQ response that wastes the anti-social seller's time and effort.

And let us not forget that time is money…

Part 2 – How to succeed – or at least, improve your chances

9. Have you done your homework?

It's funny, but there seems to be a fashion at the moment for unconscious incompetence. That's the only way I can explain the rash of piss-poor sales motions that wash over me on a daily basis.

I have been in sales roles, in one form or another, for thirty years or so. I have been an effective sole contributor and have led high performing sales teams. I have sold things, people and concepts. Sometimes, to be blunt, I have had little more to sell than an idea – "the sizzle, not the sausage". I have generally been successful, though I say so myself.

In all that time, I have been educated in at least half a dozen sales methodologies and written one of my own. Not one of those methodologies includes the words "spam the bastards" or any close approximation thereof.

Quite the contrary, all set great store by the need to do your legwork prior to any form of sales activity.

Some low-EQ sales drone once declared *"people buy from people"* as if it were some winning mantra; the reality is that **people with a need that they accept and must address and who have the budget and authority to do so will buy from people that they trust to provide a solution to that need in a timely manner at an appropriate cost and quality**.

That's four words vs forty-four and that very contrast neatly highlights one of the primary mistakes that the anti-social seller makes, time and time again.

There's just no substitute for legwork.

Qualification and Targeting are not dirty words; they are sensible and effective things to do to make the best use of your sales time and resource. Equally, a Value Proposition is not a list of capabilities thrown up in the air to see if one or more lands the right way up with your prospect.

The average anti-social seller relies heavily on an outmoded Feature => Function => Benefit approach to hosing their unfortunate victims down with their sales message. It might surprise you to learn that the FFB approach saw the light of day the very same year that Starsky and Hutch was first broadcast in the United States – 1975.

It was invented by IBM, also famed for another three-letter acronym sales approach – FUD, or Fear, Uncertainty and Doubt. Neither have a place in the 21st century; to be fair, they didn't really cut it in the 20th either. If you are going to try to sell, do so on a differentiated outcome basis, not a laundry list of technology scout badges.

At absolute minimum, make sure you have read your target's profile. Take on board how they describe themselves, the posts they make, the things they react to. Build a picture of them to help you tailor your approach and find a form of words that will get you noticed and responded to in a positive way.

Lesson. If you want to make a complex sell to a complex human being, take the time to find out about who they are, what they do and what they are likely to want and need BEFORE you waste your time and theirs.

10. Only Stalin could say this…

Many of the most ridiculous connect requests I receive, the ones so far wide of the mark that it makes you wonder if any intelligence at all has been involved in their creation, come from those who put far too much reliance in automated sales tools such as LinkedIn's own "Sales Navigator". Such tools have their uses, it's true, but they are far from being the last word in complex solution sales.

There is zero excuse for relying blindly upon such tools.

Consider this:

"Hi Bill, You came up as a recommended connection here on LinkedIn, so I thought it'd be great to connect. Looking forward to it! Thanks,"

Did you now?

If so, you are so terminally gullible that I have a bridge you might be interested in buying.

Here's another that combines a number of my favourite anti-social sales cliches and faux-pas:

"Hello, Bill. How are you?

I'm XXXX. B2b Lead Generation, Lead Search, Web Research, Email Search, Linkedin Search, Contact List Building, Data Entry Expert.

I will build your targeted email list using Zoominfo and Linkedin Sales Navigator. I'm Interested to work with you for your company. Have you any related Job?

Regards,"

Ah, you can't beat a bit of rich irony peppered with piss poor punctuation and a frail grasp of grammar and syntax.

And then there's this, which sums it up perfectly. I asked this particular individual why on earth they thought I would be interested in their 1990s – era sales pitch for some blatantly irrelevant service. This is the response I got:

"We were introduced by an algorithm, not manual spam search..."

Ah, of course. That makes it okay, then.

There seems to be a belief among anti-social sellers that if they scream loudly and long enough into the darkness, they will succeed. Quantity is believed to trump quality when it comes to selling stuff and being seen to be active is as important as actually closing business – see the next chapter for more detail on this.

Joseph Stalin is famously quoted as saying that *"Quantity has a quality all of it's own."* The thing is, he was talking about the Red Army and its role in saving Russia from the Nazi aggressor and ultimately marching into Berlin. He had a point, but he was talking about motivated and patriotic troops, not connect requests.

In particular, never <u>ever</u> give your reason for connection as "expanding your network" – a big network for the sake of it is not something to boast about, nor is it an end in itself.

Lesson. Spam is never the answer. Untargeted, one size fits all mailshots achieve nothing beyond making the sender look stupid and lazy and alienating the recipient. Less is always more, and it is better to make and nurture a handful of high-quality contacts than dozens of empty ones.

11. Say Cheese!!

I am the first to admit that my own LinkedIn profile is a mess; it's not entirely my fault; the platform assumes that people lead linear lives, moving serially from one employment to the next.

People like me, who have multiple balls in the air at any one time, are not well served by the one-after-the-other layout of the site. I run a couple of companies and am on the board of a third; I also chair a not-for-profit and I write thrillers – but only one of those can be at the top of my profile at any one time.

I can almost forgive people for not picking up on the subtleties of my portfolio existence, but I cannot ever forgive them for firing off a contact request without first READING MY DAMN PROFILE. I have lost count of the number of times I have been offered something that I do myself. It's not big and it's not clever.

I've already pointed out some of the crashingly awful taglines that people use. Mine is short, descriptive, factual and to the point. It has a couple of "oh really" points in it quite deliberately because they make fine ice breakers.

Except, of course, they are never picked up on and used as such by the anti-social sellers because that would require a degree of originality, empathy and some reading skills.

The last segment of the "About" part of my profile is a warning to the wise. Just after a quote that I find both trenchant and amusing (your mileage will almost certainly vary) I point out as follows:

"I do NOT accept unsolicited connect requests from anyone that I don't already know, or who is arrogant enough to send an empty request, who doesn't take the time to tell me why I should, who starts by saying that they have "come across" my profile, who tells me that *I* will benefit from connecting with *them* or who actually thinks for one nanosecond that I will buy their: explainer videos, hosting services, office space in London, virtual PA services, development services, cloud offerings, tech support, SEO services, Cryptocurrency, bespoke tailoring, fitness coaching, accounting services (including "helping SMBs to scale"), recruitment services, business development services, property investment "opportunities", new cars and, last but by no means least, lead generation "services" and lists of "hot prospects"."

It usually gets ignored, which, dear reader, is why this book exists.

But I digress. The point is that <u>if you are in a sales or business development role, your profile is your shop window</u>. It's the first thing I look at when I receive a connect request (and believe me, I look every time).

For goodness' sake, make yours clear, logical, tidy and informative. Pay attention to spelling, grammar, syntax and punctuation (I can't believe I am having to say this). Avoid smilies, graphics, acronyms that only mean anything to people who wear socks with sandals.

Above all, do something about your picture. Mine was done professionally; if you don't like it, don't blame the photographer, she had to work with the material she had. She worked with me to establish what sort of image I wanted to project and to whom and used that insight to deliver what I wanted.

You don't have to use a professional for your photo, but you should avoid:

- Children
- Coloured wigs
- Family pets
- Horses (unless a breeder or jockey)

- Being so small in the shot you look like a Borrower

- Holiday shots of any sort, particularly those involving beaches, shorts, flip flops, lary shirts and drunken friends

- Alcohol in general, including the overt influence of same

That last is a particular no-no; I'm sure in your private life you are a fun-loving party animal, but if you expect me for a nanosecond to do business with you, don't post an image taken at some boozy lunch in which you cannot even focus both eyes in the same direction you are sadly mistaken

Lesson. People are visual animals. If your profile looks a disorganised mess, they will assume you are yourself a disorganised mess. Use a profile photo that communicates professional competence, not a latent drink problem.

12. Are you in the right job?

This is an interesting thought and one backed up by empirical evidence. There are two schools of thought as to why the anti-social salesperson is so woefully poor at effective engagement and conversion. The first is that they have received no training, mentoring or guidance whatsoever and are simply thrashing around blindly.

The second, and more worrying, is that *they have actually been trained and instructed to behave like this*. It pains me to think that the latter is the case, but it is hard to believe that such wilfully unconscious incompetence could truly evolve independently in so many places and people simultaneously.

If that is the case, then by extension, whole cohorts of anti-social sellers are being directed by what can only be described as anti-social managers. I have myself had the misfortune over my long career in working for the odd (in more ways than one) boss who truly thought that "ten sales calls a day" was going to result in a pipeline full of qualified, solid deals.

If you find yourself working for a boss who mistakes light for heat, activity for progress, velocity for value or cadence for credibility, think again. If you are handed a template or a script to follow that starts:

"Hey [NAME] I'm [NAME] and I want to tell you about [INSERT PRODUCT CATALOGUE HERE]"

then I would respectfully suggest that your optimum sales motion is to market yourself to a company that both values their people and understands that customer relationships are forged through effective engagement and not punched out with a cookie cutter.

Lesson. Successful selling, particularly complex solution selling, is as much an art as a science. If you feel uncomfortable following the instructions you are given, either they are wrong or you are in the wrong place.

Time spent in a toxic job learning the wrong things is worse for your career than a period out of work spent looking for the right job in the right enterprise that enables you to learn and grow.

Afterword

Right, I've had my fun, but there is a very serious message here.

We are all trying to make a living. Those trying to sell and develop business are having a thin time at the moment.

But contrary to what you may have been told, single-channel anti-social selling is NOT the answer. Social selling itself is a laudable, sensible, positive step in the right direction and a vital part of successful B2B engagement, but what passes for it on LinkedIn and similar platforms these days is a pale pastiche of how it is supposed to be executed.

If you are being asked by your boss to behave and to act in some of the ways described in this book, it is high time you traded that boss in for a smarter model.

If you work for yourself and genuinely think that spamming random people on LinkedIn on the thinnest pretext (or none at all) is the best way to spend your time to generate business, please do yourself a favour and learn how to segment, target, articulate and engage effectively.

Let me finish with just one more example – an exchange that first started six months ago and came to a conclusion just as I was committing this book to print.

"Hi Bill,

My company helps businesses explain what they do through animated videos.

We have just launched so we are offering 50% off this month in exchange for a testimonial.

Here is some of our latest work

www.youtube.com/link

Would this be of interest to you?"

I responded as you would by now expect:

"First, congratulations on the launch of your company.

Second and in all honesty, you are totally wasting your time and effort sending out random requests like this.

You have made at least five mistakes in your approach, starting with firing blind. I do not need your services. I will never need your services. I have an in-house video capability.

A little more time spent on targeting and qualification, let alone working on your value proposition and how you articulate it may yield you greater dividends than aimlessly spamming."

A couple of days ago I received the following:

"Hi Bill, I wanted to thank you for your message it really helped me see what I was doing wrong and I've been a lot more successful because of it. If you have the time I'd be really interested in

discussing potential mentorship. I believe I'd learn a lot from you."

By Jove, he's got it. Of course I shall be happy to mentor him – because he is by his own admission already a better and more successful sales person for taking the advice I offered and there is clearly scope for him to learn and grow further.

I can teach you, too – for a price. And of course if you are willing and able to learn. You know how to get my attention on LinkedIn, don't you?

- Think about the outcome you want
- Do your research. If nothing else, read my profile
- Think about an outcome I might want, based upon the evidence before you
- Tailor your approach to me, personally
- Write your connect request in clear, unambiguous terms avoiding

exclamation marks, smiley faces, cliches, laundry lists, over-familiarity and mindless, pointless closed questions
- Be yourself, but leave the ego at home
- Avoid making me feel that you are doing me a favour in connecting with you
- Make me curious, and give me a reason to engage with you in order to satisfy that curiosity

…and above all, never, ever, ever open with *"Hey! Bill!"*

Acknowledgements

I'd just like to thank all of the anti-social sellers (who shall remain nameless) who have unwittingly provided a rich seam of material for this book; it could have been much, *much* longer…

I'd also like to thank my proof-readers; there is nothing wores than castigating ppl for there speling and grammer then making the same misstake yourself…

Cover image: Man Shouting by Gan Khoon Lay from the Noun Project.

Finally a big thanks to Libido Chafe, a true friend and ally without whose unique skills and encouragement this book would not have seen the light of day.

About the author

Bill Palmer is an experienced leader, entrepreneur, company director and agent of transformation, Freeman of the City of London, published author, prize-winning photographer, Liveryman, Rotarian and Chair of a public-private not-for-profit enterprise.

Bill spent thirty years in the big corporate world and he now describes that period as his "apprenticeship".

He has extensive experience in complex sales and delivery has developed a number of innovative Go-to-Market Initiatives. He is also the creator of a sales process for SMBs that helps them to compete effectively against much larger competitors.

Bill also writes thrillers in his spare time.

He freely admits that he doesn't suffer fools gladly and will quite happily take the piss out of anyone who still tries to sell at him after reading this book.

Printed in Great Britain
by Amazon

38186493R00050